My Special Family

A Children's Book About Open Adoption

By Kathleen Silber &
Debra Marks Parelskin

Illustrated By Andrew Denman

Open Adoption Press
P.O. Box 253
Orinda, CA 94563

ISBN 0-964-0009-1-1 (pbk.)

Book Design by Catherine Brandt, Image Press, San Leandro, CA

Printed and Bound in the United States of America

> **We dedicate this book to our own special families**
>
>
> Herb, Erik, and Sarah Silber
>
>
> Bruce, Daniel, and Michael Parelskin

Acknowledgments

We thank the following people whose ideas, creativity, and support helped make this book a reality: Andrew Denman, Mary Beth and Becky Mankowski, Cassie and Jeff Straus, Amy Garber, Tasha Gunn, Daniel and Michael Parelskin, Melissa Holden, Sarah Silber, Jean Duer, Maureen Pierce, and Pat Dorner. We also want to recognize Nancy Straus for her invaluable assistance in editing this book at its various stages.

We are especially grateful to the adopted children who read this book in its early stages and gave their valuable ideas and suggestions:

Ashley Simms
Heather Simms
Katie Kuhl
Megan Kuhl
Katie McLalan
Allison Darrow
Joey Cerletti
Brian Morgensen
Jennifer Dorner
Caitlin Hosenski
Bianca Reyna
Cruz Reyna

This book is for all of you!

Guide For Parents

Dear Parents:

My Special Family introduces the subject of open adoption as a positive and loving way of forming families. We encourage you to use this book during the preschool and elementary school years to help your child develop a healthy attitude about herself and her adoption.

There are many opportunities to personalize this book so it becomes your child's *own* story. We realize that some families maintain ongoing contact with the birthparents and others do not. The personalization pages enable you to share pictures of the birthparents, if you have them, or photos of your immediate family. The "Thoughts and Questions" section provides further opportunity to personalize this book when your child understands the concepts involved in adoption (See instructions later in this Guide.).

If your child is school age, you can assemble this book together, with your child selecting the photos. This can be a fun family project! If your child is too young or does not have the attention span or interest to do so, you can insert the photos and personalize the book before reading it to her. With young children, you may also want to use pencil, rather than ink, so your child can erase it and write her own story at an older age.

Throughout the book we have used the word "birthparents" to communicate to your child the reality of both a birthmother <u>and</u> birthfather. However, if you have no information about the birthfather, you may want to substitute the word "birthmother" when "birthparents" is mentioned, or "she" when "they" is used. We also recommend that you insert the birthparents' first names, where possible, rather than simply using the term birthparents. There are blanks throughout the book for you to insert the birthmother's or birthparents' names.

There are also pages which allow you or your child to elaborate about your/their own adoption experience. In these instances, there are options depending on whether or not you continue to have contact with the birthparents. For example, on the page which says "My birthparents love me, too, and this is how they have shown their love," you can describe the type of contact you have had over the years, special gifts, and so on; or, if there is no contact, you can give examples of the loving decision that was made at the time of the adoption.

When your open adoption includes visitation with the birthparents, we encourage all of you to read this book to your child *together!*

How to Use This Book with Your Preschool Age Child

We realize that preschool children do not, yet, have the capacity to *understand* adoption. However, there are several very important reasons for introducing the subject at this age:

(1) From the beginning, adoption should be a household word and a subject that is discussed easily in your home.

(2) Talking about adoption openly aids in YOUR comfort level with the topic.

(3) Your child will have a positive association with the word adoption, even though she does not grasp its full meaning.

(4) She will understand that the word adoption applies to her, even if she cannot pronounce it correctly, for example "I 'dopted!"

(5) This openness lays the ground work for positive self-esteem connected with the word adoption, which, in turn, facilitates understanding in the school age years.

One of your tasks as parents is to create an atmosphere which gives your child permission to ask questions about adoption. If you introduce the subject periodically and seem comfortable talking about the birthparents, your child will realize that it is okay for her to ask questions and verbalize curiosities.

We encourage you to discuss adoption with your child in a simple manner. It helps to remember that she needs concrete information at this age because she cannot grasp abstract concepts. Share photos of the birthparents so that your child has something specific to connect to the word "birthparents." *My Special Family* will help you do this.

Also, it is important to emphasize the permanence of your family. For example, this book conveys that you are a "forever" family and that you will "love me for always." As you discuss adoption, remember to talk positively about the birthparents because whatever you say about them reflects upon the child herself. Positive language about birthparents sets the tone for positive self-esteem and understanding about adoption.

At this stage, your child begins to question if she grew in Mommy's body. You want to convey that all children come into the world the same way, but there are many ways to join the family. Otherwise, adopted children may feel very different when they realize that they did not grow in your body (Some preschoolers have even worried that they were "aliens" because they thought they did not grow in anyone's body!). Since magical thinking is very common at this age, you need to provide accurate information.

Preschool children are not able to understand the circumstances which led the birthparents to make an adoption plan. It is usually sufficient to explain that they were unable to parent the child, and wait until the early school age years to explain why. However, if your preschooler asks, give a brief and simple explanation.

As you discuss these questions and issues with your child, we encourage you to find other ways to personalize this book. After all, the best story in the world to any young child is 'the story of how you got me!'

How to Use This Book with Your School-Age Child

As your child's level of understanding increases during the school age years, it is necessary to discuss several important issues:

(1) At this age, focus on the *circumstances* of why the birthparents made an adoption plan. As in the pre-school years, use concrete examples. This age group struggles to understand *why* they were placed for adoption, and there is a tendency to blame themselves (for example, "I was an ugly baby," "a bad baby," "I cried too much," and so on).

Your child needs to understand that the decision was based on the birthparents' circumstances and that they were not able to parent ANY child. This removes the burden of responsibility from your child.

(2) Grief is an issue at this age (typically ages 5-8). Suddenly your child realizes that she lost someone—that she had another set of parents before you—and she grieves for this loss. This is *normal!* She will experience stages of grieving (anger, depression, and so on) similar to adjusting to the death of a loved one. Your child will be able to work through this stage if you can help her verbalize these feelings.

(3) Permanency is also an issue at this age. It is important to stress the permanence of adoption and your family. Explain the commitment involved in being a family.

(4) Once your child understands why she was adopted, the next logical question is "My birthmother's circumstances have probably changed by now (For example, she is no longer 16 and too young to parent.) and maybe she could take me back." So you need to address the permanency issue not only from your perspective, but also from the birthparents' perspective.

You can discuss that the birthparents knew that your child needed a "forever" family from the beginning, that they could not be a forever family at that time due to their circumstances, which is why they selected you to be her parents. You want to reassure her that the birthparents knew that this was a permanent decision at the time of the adoption and that they still agree with it.

When contact is ongoing with the birthparents, they can provide concrete reassurance to your child of the permanence of your family. That is, even though the birthmother may have gotten married and had other children, she is not going to take your daughter back! The birthmother can say something such as "I wish I could have been your forever Mommy, but I couldn't, and that is why I picked your Mommy and Daddy to be your parents." This type of statement removes any further worry about the permanence of your family and is one of the benefits of open adoption and ongoing contact. Therefore, you may want to encourage the birthparents' participation in this discussion, either in person, on the telephone, or in letters.

Without this type of reassurance many children develop fears about the birthparents changing their minds and taking them back. They may even worry about being kidnapped, which is a very scary thought and one which many children are even too fearful to verbalize. They worry about losing their Mommy and Daddy (in effect, their whole world). After all, this happened to them once before, and they do not yet fully understand why.

(5) School-age children do not want to be *different* from their peers. Explain that your child is not different, but there are numerous ways in which families are formed. Once in school, your child will meet children with other family configurations, for example step families, blended families, and so on. At that point adoption, especially open adoption, may not seem so unusual in today's world!

However, do not be surprised if there are times during this age when your child may not want to discuss her adoption with others. You can respect her wishes for privacy, while still communicating openly within your family about adoption.

How to Use This Book If You Do Not Have Ongoing Contact with the Birthparents

Although this book was written with the assumption that many families maintain an ongoing relationship with the birthfamily, it can be used even if this is not the case. When the birthparents are involved in your life, it is easier for your child to understand adoption because her birthparents are *real* people. However, if there is no contact, you still want to convey the birthparents' love and caring, as well as provide whatever concrete information you have available.

For example, you can explain that the birthparents *showed* their love by finding the very best parents for her. This is also a wonderful opportunity to bring out any special gifts that the birthparents may have given at the time of the adoption, such as a hand-knitted baby blanket.

We find that when children do not have contact with the birthparents, it is often difficult for them to believe that the birthparents care about them. They may also interpret the lack of contact as rejection. Some children internalize this rejection, resulting in low self-esteem. We encourage you to use this book to help your child learn of the love and caring that was involved in the adoption decision and to enable her to verbalize her feelings and curiosities.

If you have limited or no contact with your child's birthparents and this is upsetting to her, we suggest that you encourage her to write a letter to the birthparents, expressing her feelings and questions. Even if this letter is not mailed, it can be beneficial. If you wish, your child can use the "Thoughts and Questions" section at the end of the book for this purpose.

How to Use the "Thoughts & Questions" Section At The End of the Book

The last two pages of the book may be used when your school age child is ready to write more in-depth questions and thoughts about adoption. It is up to you and your child to determine the best time and use for these pages. Here are some suggestions for you to consider:

(1) Your child can list the questions she has about her birthparents and the adoption decision, and you can discuss the answers together.

(2) Your child can write a letter to her birthparents.

(3) These pages can be used as a diary so that your child may freely express her thoughts and feelings about adoption.

We hope that this book will provide the *beginning* of many discussions in your home about your child's adoption. You may also want to refer to this Guide from time to time over the years as new issues arise and your child's understanding grows.

We feel fortunate to be part of the rapidly growing trend toward open adoption. We hope that *My Special Family* will have a positive impact on a generation of healthy adopted children.

Sincerely,

Kathleen and Debra
1994

My name is _____ .

This is the story of my adoption

and how it all began...

Insert baby photo

This is a picture of me when I was

a tiny baby.

My life started with my birthparents.
I grew in a special place inside of my
birthmother's body, called a womb.

My birthparents' names are _____

and _____. This is what they

look like:

Insert photo or write physical description

My birthparents _____ and

_____ love me very much.

They were sad that they could not raise

me. So they chose my Mommy and

Daddy to adopt me.

Adoption means that Mommy and Daddy are my FOREVER parents. My birthparents were happy because they found just the right Mommy and Daddy to take care of me and love me for always.

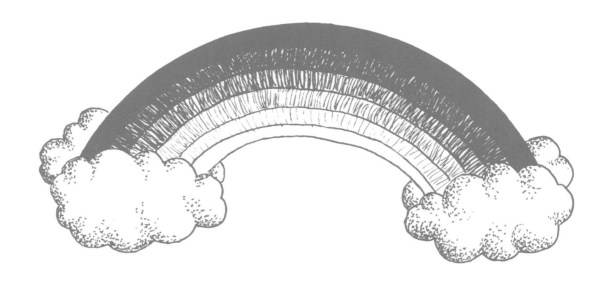

Insert photo of adoptive parents

Mommy and Daddy were sad because a baby did not grow in Mommy's body. They wanted a child to love and to raise more than anything else in the world.

Mommy and Daddy were so
excited when they were chosen by

_____

to be my parents.

Mommy and Daddy first met my
birthparents at:

_____

_____

Everyone was nervous meeting for
the first time, but they liked each
other a lot.

These are some of the things they
talked about: _____

_____

_____

_____

_____

Insert photo of this meeting, other photo of
adoptive parents and birthparents together,
or write further description of the initial meeting

Everyone was very excited when I was born, but I don't remember a thing!

I was born on this great day:

_____

at this terrific place:

_____.

Here are some other details of my birth:

_____

_____

_____

_____

Insert photo from hospital, preferably one
with birthparents,
adopting parents, and baby together.
If you do not have a photo, write a description of
the hospital experience.

When it was time to leave the hospital, my birthmother _____ gave me a special hug. Then Mommy and Daddy took me home. They were <u>so</u> happy!

When we got home, lots of friends and relatives were excited to come and see me. There are many people who love me. I know who they are:

_____

_____

_____

_____

_____

_____

That's a lot of love!

My birthparents love me, too, and this
is how they have shown their love:

_____

_____

_____

_____

_____

_____

_____

_____

_____

_____

_____

These are some of their interests
or favorite activities:

_____

_____

_____

_____

_____

And these are some of the things I
would like my birthparents to know
about me:

_____

_____

_____

Mommy and Daddy are my forever parents! We love each other very much. These are some of the fun things we do together:

_____

_____

_____

_____

_____

_____

_____

_____

_____

_____

_____

_____

This is the story of my adoption and how we will always be a family!

Insert family photo

More Thoughts and Questions

Here are some thoughts and questions I have about my adoption:

_____

_____

_____

_____

_____

_____

_____

_____

_____

_____

_____

_____

_____

_____

_____

_____

_____

_____

_____

_____

_____

_____

_____

_____

_____

_____

_____

_____

My Adoption Story to Be Continued!...

About the Authors

Kathleen Silber was born and raised in Stockton, California, graduated from the University of California at Davis, and received her Master's degree in Social Welfare from the University of California at Berkeley. She is the co-author of *Dear Birthmother* and *Children of Open Adoption* and is nationally known (including numerous national media appearances) for her pioneering work in open adoption. Kathleen and her husband and two children live in California, where she is the Associate Executive Director of the Independent Adoption Center in Pleasant Hill.

Debra Marks Parelskin was born and raised in Milwaukee, Wisconsin. She graduated from the University of Michigan and received her Master's degree in Social Work from the University of Wisconsin. Debra has worked for twelve years in the field of adoption and foster care and most recently worked with Kathleen at the Independent Adoption Center. She lives in California with her husband and two children.